backstage *pass*

Backstage at an
ANIMATED SERIES

Danny Fingeroth

Children's Press®
A Division of Scholastic Inc.
New York / Toronto / London / Auckland / Sydney
Mexico City / New Delhi / Hong Kong
Danbury, Connecticut

Special thanks to Jerome Hyman and Pomann Sound, New York, NY

Book Design: Daniel Hosek and Christopher Logan
Contributing Editor: Matthew Pitt
Photo Credits: Cover, p. 15, Cartoon Network/courtesy Everett Collection;
pp. 4, 7, 16, 19, 23, 24 Everett Collection; pp. 8, 34 © Hulton Deutsch
Collection/Corbis; p. 10 © Bettmann/Corbis; p. 13 © Hulton/Archive/Getty
Images; p. 21 Walt Disney Company/courtesy Everett Collection; p. 28 Cindy
Reiman; pp. 31, 39 Adriana Skura; p. 33 Walt Disney Company/Pixar/courtesy
Everett Collection; p. 36 © Reuters NewMedia Inc./Corbis; p. 41 courtesy Cartoon
Art Museum, San Francisco, California

Library of Congress Cataloging-in-Publication Data

Fingeroth, Danny.
  Backstage at an animated series / Danny Fingeroth.
  p. cm. — (Backstage pass)
  Summary: Explores how animation works, how animated films are
  produced and who is best known for making them, and how to
  pursue one's interest in the field, either as a career or as a hobby.
  Includes index.
  ISBN 0-516-24323-3 (lib. bdg.) — ISBN 0-516-24385-3 (pbk.)
  1. Animation (Cinematography)—Juvenile literature.
  [1. Animation (Cinematography)] I. Title. II. Series.

  TR897.5 .F55 2003
  791.43'3—dc21

                                                    2002007282

CONTENTS

It's no fairy tale: Animated movies such as *Shrek* have become the talk of Hollywood.

Introduction

Each Saturday morning, kids around the United States wake up early, even though there's no school bus to catch. They flip on the television to watch their favorite cartoon characters battle against evil or solve puzzling mysteries. Animated cartoons aren't just kids' stuff, though. Since 1989, millions of adults have spent a half-hour each Sunday watching *The Simpsons*. They roar with laughter as Homer and his family find themselves in the silliest situations. This interest in cartoons has made animated movies, such as *Toy Story* and *Shrek,* big screen blockbusters.

Generations of people have been entertained by the art of animation. Animators trick our eyes into believing we are seeing motion when we really aren't. Animators can show us wondrous things we can never see in real life, such as characters that can bend and move in impossible ways.

Animation is a serious art form. Good animators must be disciplined and patient while working on their craft. For instance, if you're watching Daffy Duck raise his hand, the on-screen action may take only one second. Animators, however, may have had to create as many as twenty-four drawings to show that brief, simple action. Dozens—even hundreds—of creative minds must work together to complete an animated world. This book will show you how the magic works. It will take you behind the scenes of an animated series. It will even give you some tips on how to become part of the magic act!

It takes the talents and energy of many people to bring your favorite cartoon characters to life.

Thomas Edison's Kinetoscope allowed the world to see photographic images in a whole new way.

CHAPTER ONE

Historic Movements

People have always told stories through pictures. Ancient cave paintings found in France show a sequence of pictures that tell a story. Ancient Egyptians drew pictures inside pyramids of important events. Through the years, peoples' need to tell stories has stayed the same. It's *how* the stories are told that has changed. Animation is an important part of that storytelling tradition.

Thomas Edison's 1893 invention, the Kinetoscope, got the ball rolling. Edison put still photographs of people and things on a roll of film. The film was put inside the Kinetoscope and viewed through a small peephole. As the film moved from one spool to another, an illusion of movement by the people in the photographs was created. The only problem was that only one person at a time could see these images.

Although Winsor McCay (far right) created a legendary animated character in *Gertie the Dinosaur*, he didn't exactly work in glamorous conditions, as this photo proves.

Enter French inventor Louis Lumière. Lumière improved Edison's machine in 1894. He found a way to project his images onto a screen. Now, many people could see moving images at once. Lumière's invention used many photos taken one right after the other. These still images were shown at sixteen frames per second, creating the illusion that they were moving. This is the basis on which all motion pictures work—even those we see today!

In 1906, James Stuart Blackton made a film called *Humorous Phases of Funny Faces*. The characters of this short film were not actors. They were drawings made by Blackton. This film is considered the first animated cartoon ever. Winsor McCay's *Gertie the Dinosaur*, made in 1914, was another cartoon milestone. This animated film was one of the first to give a personality to its title character.

People were starting to see the potential of cartoons. An industry had been born.

Trade Secret

The earliest animated cartoons shown in movie theaters were known as "shorts." Audiences watched them before the main feature began. The first full-length, animated feature wasn't made until 1937. The feature was *Snow White and the Seven Dwarfs*.

Cartoon Heroes

In the early days of animation, a handful of pioneers launched the industry. These visionary leaders included Walt Disney, the Warner Brothers, and Walter Lantz. They created techniques and tricks that survive to this day.

These pioneers also created strong stories. The stories featured characters with personality and charm. When you watched these characters, you felt for them. You wanted Bugs Bunny to get his way. You wanted Tweety to fly away from Sylvester's grasp.

A Parade of Stars

In 1928, Walt Disney made the first animated cartoon with sound. It was called "Steamboat Willie." Its star was a clever, fun-loving mouse named Mickey. Mickey Mouse became an overnight sensation.

Suddenly, audiences all over the world wanted to see cartoons on the big screen. Other animation companies were eager to please. Soon, characters such as Woody Woodpecker and Popeye the Sailor were making millions of people laugh. Other

Walt Disney's magic helped create a kingdom of unforgettable characters. Mickey Mouse is certainly his most famous animated star.

favorites, such as Superman, leapt from comic books to the big screen in a single bound.

The first TV broadcasts in the United States began in 1939. It was only a matter of time before television became the new home for animation. Audiences no longer had to travel to movie theaters to see their beloved cartoons. They could watch the cartoons in their own homes. Eventually, new cartoon characters were created specially for television. These included Yogi Bear, Huckleberry Hound, and Rocky and Bullwinkle.

Today's top TV cartoon characters include new rascals such as the Rugrats. They also feature classic heroes, such as Spider-Man. Popular animated series include *The Simpsons* and *The Powerpuff Girls*. These series appeal to a wide range of people. Children watch them for the bright colors and exciting action. Adults enjoy the clever scripts and the talented artists' drawings.

Each second of an animated film requires a total of twenty-four still images. Each image is slightly different from the one that came before, and the one that will follow. Also, each picture must be created from scratch. Many people are needed to draw and photograph these images. In this way, the process works like an assembly line. Each person has their own task to fulfill. The finished product is the result of each person fulfilling his or her task well.

Animation, however, isn't limited to hand drawings. As computers have become more useful, some

The three Powerpuff Girls—Bubbles, Blossom, and Buttercup—delight audiences as they defend Townsville from evil.

animators now use them to create their art. Other animators use clay figurines in their work. Some movies have even mixed real-life actors with cartoon creations. The art of animation is definitely on the move.

Animation certainly found a reason to celebrate in the 1950s: Art Clokey's experiments with claymation.

CHAPTER TWO

Shaping the World of Animation

CHEESE WIZ

Great animators are always looking for ways to push their art to new heights. One of these animators was Art Clokey. In the 1950s, Clokey began to experiment with a new kind of animation. He used clay forms. Clokey shaped these forms to look like common objects. Then he animated them. His first masterpiece was a piece of clay made to look like a slice of Swiss cheese. Clokey subtly reshaped the "cheese" with each frame. When people watched his work, they saw what looked like bites being taken out of the slice! Clokey also invented the clay-animation, or claymation, characters Gumby and Pokey.

To create figures that seem to move, clay animators use a special clay called plastilene. Plastilene is made from an oil that keeps the clay moist and soft. Animators also use an armature.

An armature serves as the framework on which the clay can be molded. It can be something as simple as a thin wire strung through the figure. Armatures allow clay figures to be bent while holding their shapes together.

Claymation's popularity hasn't dried up over the years. Many popular commercials have used clay characters that became stars. In the mid-1980s, The California Raisins took the stage. This rock band of animated raisins delighted audiences, singing hits like "I Heard It Through the Grapevine." More recently, Lipton ice tea began to use claymation figures to promote their beverage.

Claymation requires huge amounts of patience and skill. That's why British animator Nick Park's work is so impressive. Park created the characters Wallace and Gromit. Wallace makes many odd inventions, such as mechanical trousers. Gromit is his faithful canine companion. Park has created three short Wallace and Gromit films. The first took him six years to make! In 2000, Park completed the first full-length claymation feature, *Chicken Run*.

Claymation has come a long way since Art Clokey's early work. Here, the claymation cast of *Chicken Run* hatches a scheme to escape certain doom.

CGI

As technology marches forward, animation is following right behind. In many of today's cartoons, characters and backgrounds appear almost real. Characters such as those in the series *Max Steele* and the movie *Shrek* are amazingly lifelike. This effect is created thanks to computer generated images (CGIs). Special computer programs may be used to enhance animation. The artists, though, still have to start from scratch.

Let's say an animator was trying to create a CGI of a rabbit's face. The animator would connect simple lines and points to show the rabbit's long, floppy ears. At this point, the face would only be a series of straight and curving lines. This first image is called a wireframe. That's because the object looks like it was made out of wire.

The CGI is then shaded in gray. This allows animators to begin to see the shape and definition of their CGI. After the rabbit is shaded, the computer animator renders it. Rendering a CGI means that the animator smoothes out the bumps. For instance, if the rabbit's nose looks too pointed, the rendering can round it out. Also, during the rendering process, the animator adds shadows and light to the object.

Finally, it's time to put the CGI in motion. The idea behind CGI animation is the same as drawn animation. The animators are trying to convince audiences that still pictures are moving. The great thing about CGIs is that they provide more than the illusion of movement. They provide an illusion of depth.

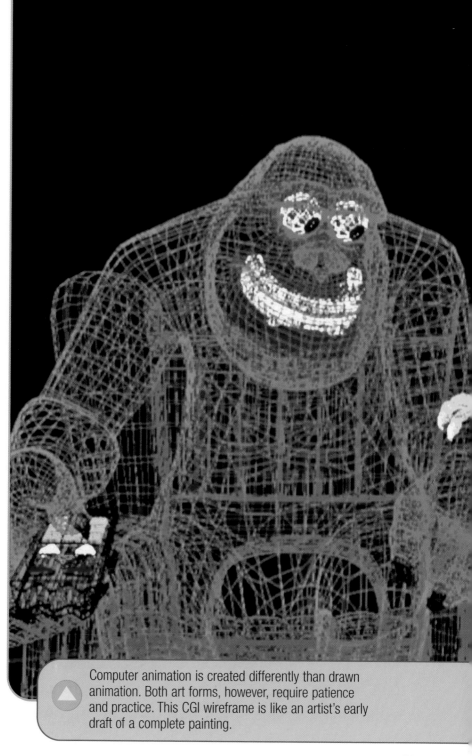

Computer animation is created differently than drawn animation. Both art forms, however, require patience and practice. This CGI wireframe is like an artist's early draft of a complete painting.

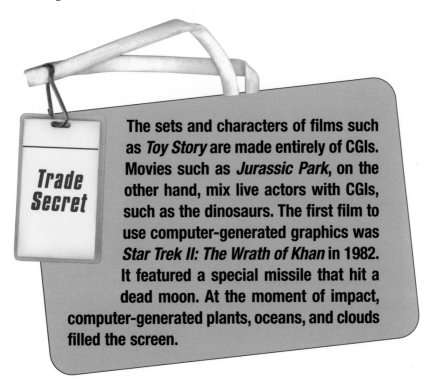

Trade Secret

The sets and characters of films such as *Toy Story* are made entirely of CGIs. Movies such as *Jurassic Park*, on the other hand, mix live actors with CGIs, such as the dinosaurs. The first film to use computer-generated graphics was *Star Trek II: The Wrath of Khan* in 1982. It featured a special missile that hit a dead moon. At the moment of impact, computer-generated plants, oceans, and clouds filled the screen.

Make Us Care

In some ways, whether the animation is drawn, sculpted, or created on a computer screen doesn't really matter. The most important element of good animation is a great story. Audiences need to care about the characters they watch. A cartoon character might be able to bend, stretch, and bounce. Yet if the character has no personality, it probably won't move the viewer. Story is especially important for an animated series, which features the same characters day after day, or week after week.

Dinosaurs may be extinct, but Hollywood has been able to "reanimate" them in films, thanks to the magic of computer generated images.

To create an original, exciting story line each week, teams of television animators must perform some heroic feats.

CHAPTER THREE

Movers and Shakers

You know that an animated cartoon is made up of thousands of drawings. You also know that these drawings are shown quickly, one after another, creating an illusion of movement. A TV audience, however, would get bored just watching thousands of random drawings on the screen. How do all the drawings get shaped into an exciting, half-hour animated series?

FIRST, THE STORY

Before animators can start drawing, they have to know what to draw. So the first step in putting an animated show on the air deals with words, not pictures. A writer working on a series makes up a story. For example, if the series is *The Simpsons*, this story will revolve around a member of the family. Often, an episode of *The Simpsons* focuses on Homer, the father of the family. Originally, the show focused equally on all five of the Simpson family members. Over time, however, Homer's outrageous antics began to take center stage. This will often happen in an animated series. A character that stands out in a large cast will naturally claim the spotlight.

The writer first describes the story idea to producers. The producers decide if this story is right for the character. They ask questions: Has a similar story been done before? Are the characters acting like an audience would expect them to act? For example, fans of *The Simpsons* know that Homer loves junk food. So a story showing Homer eating carrots instead of hamburgers wouldn't make sense. However, what if Homer found out he had to lose weight or he'd be fired? Then it would make sense that he was skipping that burger!

If the producers like the story idea, the writer will create a first draft of the script. The draft is presented in a special script format. The script format details the action the writer wishes to see in the story. This format will give direction to the art staff, so they'll know what to draw. The script also

Trade Secret

Episodes for an animated series are often written in a team manner. One writer may write a script's first draft on his or her own. Since animated TV series have such tight deadlines, however, they often need several writers to polish that script.

provides the characters' dialogue. The rest of the writing staff then reads the first draft. Everyone adds ideas to help make the script as entertaining as possible. Before it reaches its final stage, a script will go through many rewrites.

FINDING A VOICE

Once the final script is approved, actors are brought into a recording studio. They read the script's dialogue. It may seem odd to do this *before* the artwork is created. You might expect that the drawing would be done first, and the voices added later. Actually, it's much easier to sync, or adapt, the pictures to the words than the other way around. This process helps animators match the characters' expressions and gestures to the actors' sounds. Let's say Homer has just dropped a donut

Before artists can draw the images of a cartoon character such as Homer howling, an actor must provide the sound of that painful howl.

into a fish tank. As he reaches to pull the donut out, a fish bites his hand. The actor performing Homer's voice lets out a long howl to show that Homer is in deep pain. The animators will listen carefully to this howl. They'll figure out just how to animate Homer's mouth. The length of Homer's howl will also tell them how many pictures they need to draw.

In Japanese cartoons that are dubbed for English-speaking audiences, such as *Pokémon*, characters' words don't always match the shapes their mouths are making. This is because the cartoon was originally created from a Japanese script. English words were dubbed in later. What might be a short sentence in English could be a long one in Japanese.

As the dialogue is being recorded, some basic art is being prepared. For instance, if a new character is introduced in the story, a designer will sketch what this character looks like. The designer will draw several different poses of this new character, creating what is known as a model sheet. The same thing is done for a new setting. For instance, if a circus is part of the story, an artist will design the circus.

Trade Secret

For many reasons, cartoon characters may go through makeovers. Some of Bugs Bunny's antics used to "bug" Bugs's viewers. So the Warner Brothers studio decided that Bugs's playfulness should be less annoying. Also, they asked animators to redraw him, to reflect his gentler nature. Characters may also be updated to reflect contemporary art tastes. If you compare today's Batman cartoons to those of the 1970s, you'd hardly recognize the Dark Knight!

Storyboards

After the dialogue is recorded, it's time to draw storyboards. Storyboards are the animators' road map. They look a lot like comic strips. Storyboards break the script down into a series of many small, still pictures. These pictures show how the action described in the script should look in the final cartoon. The script's dialogue is usually written under the pictures of the storyboard. The storyboarding process has become the standard way of making animation. It was popularized by the Walt Disney Studios in the 1940s.

STEP BY STEP

Once the storyboards are finished, the pencil artists can do their job. These artists draw the key, or main, actions in a cartoon. For instance, if Bart Simpson is skateboarding down a hill, the pencil artist will draw Bart at the top, middle, and bottom of this hill.

Storyboard artists sketch out what the main actions of an animated series should look like.

Since animation is made up of twenty-four separate images per second, there are still many drawings that need to be created. These are drawn by artists called in-betweeners. You might be able to guess what their job is. In-betweeners create the many drawings that fit "in between" the key actions.

After the pencil-line drawings of the moving characters are created, they are traced over in ink using a brush or a pen. These inked drawings are then transferred to clear plastic sheets. These illustrated sheets are called cels.

Next, each cel is colored. The colors add energy and richness to the previously black-and-white images. The colors can be painted in with a brush. Today, though, animators are frequently using computers, not brushes, to color their artwork.

Backgrounds are the scenery over which animated characters appear to move. They are usually drawn on some type of artboard, similar to the ones used in schools. Some backgrounds, however, can be as simple as a sheet of white paper. For an animated series, the backgrounds are usually more elaborate.

The cels are carefully placed over the background. They are then photographed—one cel at a time.

The illusion of depth and perspective provided by *Toy Story's* CGIs can't be achieved in simple cell animation.

The equipment used in early animation projects is nowhere near as reliable and efficient as the devices that are used today.

For instance, animators end up with many still photos of Bart Simpson skateboarding down the hill. Each still frame differs ever so slightly from the one before. When the stills are viewed by audiences, they see the smooth motion of Bart zooming along.

Timing Is Everything

An important part of making a cartoon is timing. Timing determines how many frames each action will take. If Bart is skating down the hill very fast, fewer frames will be needed to show his action. If he's just strolling slowly, more frames will be needed. Special timing sheets and computer programs help animators figure out exactly how long each scene will take to play out. Timing lets animators know just how many separate drawings each action will require. Perfect timing gives the series of frames a great flow.

Matt Groening's most famous creation, *The Simpsons*, has been a critical hit for years. It didn't happen overnight, though. Matt has been drawing cartoons and sketches since the age of six!

CHAPTER FOUR

A Career Come to Life!

By now, you might be pretty excited about cartoons. You may even be dreaming of making cartoons for a living. There are many ways to try out these dreams.

FLIP FOR IT

Making a flipbook is the easiest way to animate. It can be done with a simple stack of index cards. Take the first card off the stack. Draw an image on it—anything you like. You should start with something simple, such as a circle. On the next card, draw another circle. It should be the same size as the first. However, you should draw this second circle a tiny bit to the right of where you drew the first. Keep doing this for about twenty cards. When you finish, hold the stack at the end farthest from the drawings. With your thumb, flip the edges of the cards on the drawn ends. Your circle will appear to move. That's all there is to it. You've made an animated cartoon! You can use more complex drawings in your next flipbook.

CLAIM TO FRAME

You can make more than flipbooks using stacks of index cards. You can even animate your first film. You'll need an old super 8mm or 16mm camera (or a video camera) to complete this project. On your stack of index cards, make a bunch of drawings of the same image in slightly different positions. Using your camera, click one or two frames of each drawing at a time. When you play back the film or video, you'll see the images move. With practice, you'll learn how many frames are needed to make an image move faster or slower.

You might have fun animating objects instead of drawings. Try animating a toy car moving across a table or desk. Shoot a couple frames of the car at its original position. Move the car 1/4 inch. Shoot a couple frames of the car at this position. Repeat the process, moving the car 1/4 inch each time. When you play back the film or video, the car will appear to be driving. Be sure that your fingers are out of the frame!

BE A LEARNING INTERN

The next time you watch your favorite animated series, stick around for the credits. Look for the names of the studios that worked on the series. Those studios need smart, talented interns. Most major animation studios are in California. Many towns, however, have small studios that do animated commercials for local companies. Contact the human resources departments at studios close to you. Tell them you're willing to be an intern. You may be able to get school credit for your work, or even a small paycheck.

The main benefit, however, is experience. You will get to learn from animators and impress them with your talents. They may even hire you at some point down the road.

Working as an intern for an animation studio can really pay off. Young interns get to learn their trade from the finest cartoonists, while drawing on their impressive wisdom and experience.

CARTOONS IN A FLASH

In recent years, a process called Flash animation has become popular. Flash animation uses software that lets users animate drawings on their computers. Flash is making a splash on Web sites. Some TV cartoons have begun to use Flash, too. Flash cartoons are often cheaper to make than regular animation. Many of them require only a couple of artists, instead of a studio full of animators. If you buy the software, you can learn Flash, too. It's an expensive investment, though—Flash software costs about $400.

JOIN THE CLUB

Why not get together with a bunch of friends who enjoy animation? You could start a club to make and discuss cartoons. You can take turns with the many jobs that go into making a cartoon. One week, one person could write, another could draw, and a third could run the camera. The next week, you can all switch tasks.

VISIT A MUSEUM

Some museums, such as San Francisco's Cartoon Art Museum, are entirely devoted to comics and

Some of animation's finest moments have been enshrined and honored in the Cartoon Art Museum.

animation. Many other museums have exhibits about cartoons. The exhibits bring the history of great animation to life. Other programs provide interviews by the very people who make animated cartoons. You can draw from their experience. Then you can decide if you want to follow in their footsteps!

NEW WORDS

animation a film that uses drawings or still photographs to create an illusion of movement

armature a framework, often made of wire, used to keep claymation figures from breaking apart when they're bent and twisted

cel a transparent sheet of plastic on which animators draw their art

claymation a form of animation that uses clay figures instead of drawings

computer generated image (CGI) an image that is created on a computer screen, rather than by hand

dialogue the words said by characters in a story

dubbed to have added new dialogue or sound to an animated series or film

Flash animation a form of animation created using software on a computer

flipbook a stack of index cards that, when flipped, appear to show objects moving

frame one individual picture in a film

in-betweeners animators who create the drawings that occur between major actions

Kinetoscope an early device made by Thomas Edison that displayed the illusion of movement on film

pioneers those people who are the first to do or say something important

plastilene a special, oil-based kind of clay used by claymation animators

storyboards a series of still pictures that provides animators with a blueprint of what they will draw

sync to adapt the pictures of a cartoon to fit the dialogue

timing a measure of how many frames each action will take

wireframe the earliest phase of a computer generated image; an object drawn using only lines and points

Bulloch, Ivan. *Cartoons & Animation*. Danbury, CT: Children's Press, 1999.

Schultz, Ron. *Looking Inside Cartoon Animation*. Emeryville, CA: Avalon Travel Publishing, 1992.

Tatchell, Judy. *How to Draw Cartoons and Caricatures*. New York: EDC Publications, 1990.

Viska, Peter. *The Animation Book*. New York: Scholastic, Inc., 1994.

Festivals

Fans from all over the world attend animation festivals to enjoy old and new cartoons. Often, these festivals hold competitions. If you finish a cartoon that you're proud of, enter it into a contest. Here are a couple of major festivals:

Vancouver Effects & Animation Festival
Suite 257-2906 West Broadway Avenue
Vancouver, B.C.
Canada V6K 2G8
(604) 240-4880
E-mail: veaf@sights.com

California SUN International Animation Festival
Department of Art, Mail Drop 8300
California State University Northridge
18111 Nordhoff Street
Northridge, CA 91330
(818) 382-4545
E-mail: calSUNfestival@sbcglobal.net

Web Sites

Jerry Beck's Cartoon Research
www.cartoonresearch.com
This site features a trivia page that answers many unusual questions. Find out, for instance, if Tweety is a boy or girl canary.

Animation World Network
www.awn.com
Learn the latest animation industry news, read reviews, and get career advice.

Cartoon Network.com
www.cartoonnetwork.com
This site is filled with clips from both classic cartoons and new series. It features a link to a virtual tour of the Hanna-Barbera animation studios.

INDEX

About the Author

Danny Fingeroth was the editor of Spider-Man comics for many years. He helped create the Spider-Man animated series in the mid-1990s. Danny was also the story editor on Showtime's WhirlGirl animated series. He has written hundreds of comic books and several prose novels.